ONE ROBE, ONE BOWL

Ryōkan has said:
"Who says my poems are poems?
My poems are not poems.
After you know my poems are not poems,
Then we can begin to discuss poetry!"

*And, in autograph lines on a self-
portrait sketch (see overleaf):*

"It is not that I do not wish
to associate with men,
But living alone I have the better Way."

せてゆくとしてもるくめしも
れうちの花切とここ少々
少々く川やは里くへ川
里て山里くれくは
まてく九
5

Weatherhill
New York · Tokyo

ONE ROBE, ONE BOWL

The Zen Poetry of Ryōkan

translated and introduced by John Stevens

First edition, 1977

Published by John Weatherhill, Inc., of New York and Tokyo, with
editorial offices at 7-6-13 Roppongi, Minato-ku, Tokyo 106, Japan.
Protected by copyright under terms of the International Copyright
Union; all rights reserved. Printed and first published in Japan.

LIBRARY OF CONGRESS CATALOGING IN PUBLICATION DATA: Ryōkan,
1758–1831. / One robe, one bowl. / Includes bibliographical refer-
ences and index. / I. Title. / PL797.6.A28 1977 / 895.6'1'3 /
77-2405 / ISBN 0-8348-0125-6 / ISBN 0-8348-0126-4 pbk.

FOR JOYCE

CONTENTS

INTRODUCTION

> What will remain as my legacy?
> Flowers in the spring,
> The hototogisu in summer,
> And the crimson leaves of autumn.

In his Nobel Prize acceptance speech in 1968, the late Yasunari Kawabata* quoted the above poem of Ryōkan's and added that Ryōkan transmitted the essence and emotions of old Japan. Daisetz T. Suzuki wrote in his *Zen and Japanese Culture*, "When we know one Ryōkan, we know hundreds of thousands of Ryōkans in Japanese hearts."† Both Kawabata and Suzuki felt that Ryōkan represents something very special in the Japanese character and that therefore all who wish truly to understand Japan should study the life and poetry of this eighteenth-century hermit-monk. From a religious standpoint also, Ryōkan is exceptional, exemplifying as he does the Zen Buddhist idea of attaining enlightenment and then returning to the world with "a serene face and gentle words." In his life he was indeed Daigu, the "Great Fool" (the literary name he gave himself), one who had gone beyond the limitations of all artificial, man-made restraints.

RYŌKAN'S LIFE AND CHARACTER   Ryōkan was born some time around 1758 (the exact date of his birth is unknown) in the village of Izumozaki in Echigo province on the west coast of Japan. This area, now known as Niigata Prefecture, is rather remote even today, far removed

---

*Names of modern (post-1868) Japanese are given in the Western order, as here, while the names of pre-1868 Japanese are given in the traditional Japanese order, with family name first, e.g., Tachibana Inan.

†Daisetz T. Suzuki, *Zen and Japanese Culture*, p. 364.

from the commercial and cultural centers of Tokyo, Osaka, and Kyoto. It is "snow country" and bitterly cold in winter. Ryōkan's family was well established in the area, and his father, Tachibana Inan,* was the village headman, the local Shinto priest, and a prosperous merchant.

Ryōkan's father was a complex person with a sensitive and passionate nature. He was a haiku poet of some note, with a certain following, but also an ardent imperial supporter and opponent of the *bakufu*, the military government in Edo. The reason for his unhappiness with the government is not clear (perhaps in his duties as village headman he had some clashes with bakufu officials), but when his son Yoshiyuki succeeded him (Ryōkan was the oldest son but turned his inheritance over to his brothers and sisters when he became a monk), Inan left home and spent many years wandering around Japan before settling in Kyoto. He again declared his support of the emperor and, evidently feeling intolerably oppressed by the bakufu, committed suicide in 1795 by throwing himself into the Katsura River in Kyoto as a protest; he was sixty years of age. Little is known of Ryōkan's mother, but it is clear from his poems concerning her that she was a very gentle and loving person. She died in 1783, and Inan left the village forever three years later.

Ryōkan's childhood name was Eizō. He was a quiet and studious boy who often spent long hours reading the *Analects* of Confucius. His family was well off, and the atmosphere in his home was a literary and religious one—two brothers and one sister also entered the Buddhist priesthood. His youth was calm and sheltered, and passed uneventfully until his eighteenth year.

---

*There is some confusion even among Japanese scholars concerning the correct name of Ryōkan's father. His family name was Araki, but when he married he was adopted into his wife's family, Yamamoto. His formal name became Yamamoto Iori, but he always referred to himself as Tachibana Inan, his literary name. The memorial stone in front of his ancestral home reads, "Birthplace of Tachibana Inan."

Ryōkan was to succeed his father as village headman when he turned eighteen. While training for the post, he found it especially trying. He was honest and conciliatory by nature and hated contention or discord of any kind, but was forced to deal with many conflicts and troublesome cases. In addition to those burdensome duties, he seems to have been undergoing some inner, spiritual crisis. Previously he had been a fun-loving young man, generous with his money and the center of attention at the local geisha parties, but he started to become withdrawn and silent in the midst of festivities.

Clearly something was troubling him, and he decided to become a Buddhist monk. In 1777 he shaved his head and entered Kōshō-ji, the local Zen temple, where he took the name Ryōkan (*ryō* means good; *kan* signifies generosity and largeheartedness). After he had trained there for about four years, a famous Zen priest known as Kokusen came to deliver a lecture. Kokusen was the abbot of Entsū-ji temple at Tamashima in Bitchū province (present-day Okayama Prefecture). Ryōkan was greatly impressed with Kokusen and decided to become his disciple and return with him to Entsū-ji. Ryōkan was then twenty-two.

He trained under Kokusen at Entsū-ji for almost twelve years. During this time he continued his studies of *waka*, Chinese poetry, linked verse, or *renga*, and calligraphy, becoming skilled in all of them. He was appointed Kokusen's chief disciple and was given a document certifying his enlightenment in 1790. The following year Kokusen died and Ryōkan left Entsū-ji to begin a series of pilgrimages that would last almost five years. After learning of his father's suicide in 1795, Ryōkan went to Kyoto and held a memorial service for him. He then decided to return to his native village.

After searching for a time, he found an empty hermitage halfway up Mount Kugami, about six miles from his ancestral home. He named it Gogō-an. *Gogō* is half a *shō*, the amount of rice necessary to sustain a man for one day; *an* is hermitage. It is this period of Ryōkan's life—extending from his establishment of Gogō-an at the age of forty to his death thirty-four years later—that is the most remarkable.

While his hermitage was deep in the mountains, he often visited the neighboring villages to play with the children, drink sakè with the farmers, or visit his friends. He slept when he wanted to, drank freely, and frequently joined the dancing parties held in summer. He acquired his simple needs by mendicancy, and if he had anything extra he gave it away. He never preached or exhorted, but his life radiated purity and joy; he was a living sermon.

He respected everyone and bowed whenever he met anyone who labored, especially farmers. His love for children and flowers is proverbial among the Japanese. Often he spent the entire day playing with the children or picking flowers, completely forgetting his begging for that day. If anyone asked him to play the board game *go* or recite some of his poems, he would always comply. He was continually smiling, and everyone he visited felt as if "spring had come on a dark winter's day."

When he was sixty he moved to a small hermitage next to Otogo Shrine, and at sixty-nine, due to ill health, he went to live with his disciple Kimura Motoemon. It was in the Kimura residence in Shimazaki that he first met his famous disciple, the nun Teishin.

Teishin was forty years Ryōkan's junior. She had been married to a physician when seventeen or eighteen, but he died several years later and she became a nun at the age of twenty-three. She was twenty-nine when she met Ryōkan, and they seem to have fallen in love almost immediately. They delighted in each other's company, composing poems and talking about literature and religion for hours. She was with him when he died on January 6, 1831. One of his last verses reads:

> Life is like a dewdrop,
> Empty and fleeting;
> My years are gone

12

And now, quivering and frail,
I must fade away.

Four years later, in 1835, Teishin published a collection of Ryōkan's poems entitled *Hasu no tsuyu* (Dewdrops on a lotus leaf). Teishin devoted herself to Ryōkan's memory until her death in 1872.

There are many stories and anecdotes concerning Ryōkan's eccentric behavior. Following are a few of the most famous.

Kameda Hōsai, a famous scholar who lived in Edo (now Tokyo), once went to visit Ryōkan. He found the way to Ryōkan's hermitage, but when he reached it Ryōkan was sitting in zazen on the veranda. Hōsai, not wishing to disturb him, waited until he finished almost three hours later. Ryōkan was very glad to meet Hōsai, and they talked of poetry, philosophy, and literature for the rest of the day. Evening approached, and Ryōkan wanted to get some sakè so they could continue talking. He asked Hōsai to wait a few minutes and hurried out.

Hōsai waited and waited, but Ryōkan did not return. When he could stand it no longer, he went out to try to find Ryōkan. To his astonishment, he saw Ryōkan about a hundred yards from the hermitage, sitting under a pine, gazing dreamily at the full moon. "Ryōkan! Where have you been? I've been waiting for you for more than three hours! I thought something terrible had happened to you!" Hōsai shouted.

"Hōsai-san! You have come just in time. Isn't the moon splendid?"

"Yes, yes, it's wonderful. But where is the sakè?"

"The sakè? Oh, yes, the sakè. I'm so sorry, please excuse me. I forgot all about it. Forgive me. I'll go get some right away!" Ryōkan sprang up and bounded down the path, leaving Hōsai standing in amazement.

One spring afternoon, Ryōkan noticed three bamboo shoots growing under his veranda. Bamboo grows rapidly, and soon the shoots were pressing against the bottom of the veranda.

Ryōkan was quite anxious, for he did not like anything to suffer, even plants. He cut three holes in the floor and then told the bamboo shoots not to worry; he would cut a hole in the roof if necessary. He was happy once again.

Ryōkan never preached to or reprimanded anyone. Once his brother asked Ryōkan to visit his house and speak to his delinquent son. Ryōkan came but did not say a word of admonition to the boy. He stayed overnight and prepared to leave the next morning. As the wayward nephew was lacing Ryōkan's straw sandals, he felt a warm drop of water. Glancing up, he saw Ryōkan looking down at him, his eyes full of tears. Ryōkan then returned home, and the nephew changed for the better.

Ryōkan loved to play hide-and-seek with the children. One day he ran to hide in the outhouse. The children knew where he was but decided to play a joke and run away without telling him. The next morning someone came into the outhouse and saw Ryōkan crouching in the corner. "What are you doing here, Ryōkan?" she said. "Shh, be quiet, please," he whispered, "or else the children will find me."

Once when he was walking near the village he heard a small voice cry, "Help! Help me, please!" A little boy was stuck in the topmost branches of a persimmon tree. Ryōkan helped the lad down and said he would pick some fruit for him. Ryōkan climbed the tree and picked one of the persimmons. He decided to taste it first, since unripe persimmons can be very astringent and he did not want to give one to the boy. No, it was very sweet. He picked another and it too was sweet. One after another, he stuffed the persimmons into his mouth, exclaiming, "Oh, how sweet!" He had completely forgotten about the little boy waiting hungrily below until the boy yelled, "Ryōkan! Please give me some persimmons!" Ryōkan came to his senses, laughed, and passed the delicious fruit to his small friend.

Someone told Ryōkan that if you find money on the road you will be very happy. One day, after he had received some coins during a begging trip, he decided to try it. He scattered the coins along the road and then picked them up. He did this several times but did not feel particularly happy, and he wondered what his friend had meant. He tried it a few more times and in the process lost all the money in the grass. After searching for a long time he finally found all the money he had lost. He was very happy. "Now I understand," he thought; "to find money on the road is indeed a joy."

Ryōkan's tomb is located in Shimazaki, and his hermitage still stands on Mount Kugami. There is a small temple on the cliff overlooking the Japan Sea where Ryōkan's boyhood home once stood, and an art museum and memorial hall dedicated to him have been erected near Izumozaki. Many people come each year to visit these sites associated with Ryōkan, one of Japan's most beloved poets.

RYŌKAN AND ZEN   Ryōkan was a monk of the Sōtō Zen sect, which was brought to Japan from China by Dōgen (1200–1253), the founder of Eihei-ji monastery in Fukui Prefecture, the largest and most famous monastery in Japan. Dōgen's teaching emphasized two main points: (1) *shikantaza*, themeless sitting in zazen, that is, abandoning all thoughts of good or bad, enlightenment or illusion, and just sitting; and (2) *shushō ichigyō*, "practice and enlightenment are one." There is no sudden enlightenment, and enlightenment cannot be separated from one's practice. For these reasons, Sōtō Zen is usually contrasted with Rinzai Zen, with its use of kōans during zazen and its striving for *kenshō*, an instantaneous, profound insight into reality. Generally speaking, Rinzai Zen tends to be somewhat violent and severe, while Sōtō Zen is usually more restrained and quiet.

As a Sōtō Zen monk, Ryōkan first followed the traditional pattern of communal life in the monastery, then a period as an *unsui*, a pilgrim monk drifting from place to place like "clouds and water" (*unsui*) visiting other masters. Ryōkan could have become the head of a temple or taken some other position in a large monastery, but he was not interested. His severe training had made him not austere or remote but more open and kind. Therefore, he "returned to the marketplace with bliss-bestowing hands," the state depicted in the last of the well-known Zen series of the ten oxherding pictures, and the culmination of all Buddhist practice.

Ryōkan's life at Gogō-an represents that highest stage of Zen spirituality very well. He mingled with all types of people, living Zen without preaching about it. He was detached from his detachment, free of any sort of physical or spiritual materialism; in love with nature, he was sensitive to all the myriad forms of human feeling.

> With no-mind, blossoms invite the butterfly;
> With no-mind, the butterfly visits the blossoms.
> When the flower blooms, the butterfly comes;
> When the butterfly comes, the flower blooms.
> I do not "know" others,
> Others do not "know" me.
> Not-knowing each other we naturally follow the Way.

In this famous poem "no-mind" is *mushin*, the mind that abides nowhere, the mind free of contrivance. No-mind has no obstructions or inhibitions and therefore is synonymous with Zen. "Know" here means to categorize or analyze oneself and others. Throughout Ryōkan's poems we find this theme: "Don't cling! Don't strive! Abandon yourself! Look beneath your feet!"

The other Buddhist element strongly felt in Ryōkan's poems is *mujō*, impermanence. This world is a dream, passing away like dew.

> Long ago, I often drank sakè at this house;
>   now only the earth
> Covered with plum blossoms.

16

Ryōkan's Zen is replete with *mushin*, the mind without cal-
culation or pretense, and *mujō*, the sense of the impermanence
of all things.

RYŌKAN'S POEMS Ryōkan wrote in many different styles of
poetry—classical Chinese, haiku, waka,
folk songs, and *Man'yō*-style poems. The Chinese poems, or
kanshi, generally contain five Chinese characters per line, al-
though some lines have seven characters, with a minimum of
four lines. Most of the poems are untitled. There are about
four hundred of these Chinese poems. In both his life style and
his Chinese poems Ryōkan is often compared to the famous
eighth-century Chinese poet Han-shan (Kanzan), the eccentric
hermit of Cold Mountain. Ryōkan often read Han-shan's
poems, and the work of both men has a fresh, "country"
feeling with little ornamentation.

Ryōkan frequently ignored rules of literary composition in
writing his Japanese-style poems; consequently, many of his
haiku (three lines of five, seven, and five syllables, respectively)
and waka (five lines of five, seven, five, seven, and seven syl-
lables, respectively) do not conform to the classical pattern.
Actually, the number of haiku is quite small, the majority of
his Japanese poems being free-style waka. He also composed a
few folk songs and a number of *Man'yō*-style poems (the style
used in the *Man'yōshū*, an eighth-century collection of ancient
Japanese poetry) with many syllables. He wrote about one
thousand Japanese-style poems altogether.

Most of the poems are concerned with Ryōkan's daily life—
begging for his food, playing with the children, visiting the
local farmers, walking through the fields and hills. He also
wrote love poems to Teishin and poems on Buddhist themes.

Far from being highly crafted and refined, Ryōkan's poems
are spontaneous and direct; simple and pure on the surface,
they contain a profound inner feeling of *mushin* and *mujō*. His
poems are very beautiful when chanted and are popular among

17

devotees of *shigin*, classical poetry recitation. Ryōkan is also known as one of Japan's great calligraphers, and originals of his poems are highly valued. We see, then, that Ryōkan is esteemed both for his unconventional life and for the lyrics, content, and calligraphic form of his poetry.

A NOTE ON THE   This selection of Ryōkan's poetry includes
TRANSLATIONS   100 Chinese poems and 103 Japanese poems
(101 waka and 2 haiku). The Chinese poems are arranged in no particular order or sequence; all Ryōkan's poems were collected from various sources after his death, and few of the poems can be accurately dated or chronologically arranged. As already mentioned, most of the poems were untitled; consequently, only those poems given titles by Ryōkan himself are titled in this book. There are also a few examples of poems linked under a single title. Following the Japanese custom, the waka and haiku have been grouped into five sections: spring, summer, autumn, winter, and miscellaneous.

I have deliberately avoided all refined or "poetic" expressions in rendering Ryōkan's poetry into colloquial English. His verses are fresh and direct, without ornamentation or ostentation, and I have attempted to reproduce this in my translations. The poems are generally free of abstruse literary or historical allusions, so I have added few notes. The translations of the Chinese-style poems are quite literal and follow the originals closely; the waka present more of a problem due to their brevity, but I have kept the number of extra words and phrases to a minimum.

When Teishin published the first collection of Ryōkan's poems, she stated that her purpose was not so much to present the art of Ryōkan's poetry as to make known his spirit and way of life. This is also my purpose. Ryōkan lived his poetry more than any other poet. In contrast with the great majority of Chinese bureaucratic and Japanese court poets, whose "huts" were more like villas and who spent more time involved in petty intrigue than looking at the moon, Ryōkan's poverty and simplicity were real and unaffected. Ryōkan's life and poetry were inseparable; this charm and beauty are what I hope the reader will find in my translations.

ACKNOWLEDGMENTS   I would like to express my gratitude to Joyce Stevens for helping me translate many of these poems, typing the manuscript, and making many useful suggestions. Special thanks go to Mr. Kōsen Nishiyama of the Tōhoku College of Social Welfare for his advice and general encouragement, and to Ms. Suzanne Trumbull of Weatherhill, who was a most considerate and helpful editor. I would also like to thank Mr. Meredith Weatherby of Weatherhill for taking an interest in Ryōkan and supporting the publication of this book.

Finally, I wish to thank the Ryōkan Kinen-kan (Ryōkan Memorial Collection) in Izumozaki, Niigata Prefecture, for permission to reproduce Ryōkan's self-portrait and calligraphy.

CHINESE POEMS

ONE NARROW path surrounded by a dense forest;
On all sides, mountains lie in darkness.
The autumn leaves have already fallen.
No rain, but still the rocks are dark with moss.
Returning to my hermitage along a way known to few,
Carrying a basket of fresh mushrooms
And a jar of pure water from the temple well.

～

THE RAIN has stopped, the clouds have drifted away,
　　and the weather is clear again.
If your heart is pure, then all things in your world are pure.
Abandon this fleeting world, abandon yourself,
Then the moon and flowers will guide you along the Way.

～

I SIT quietly, listening to the falling leaves—
A lonely hut, a life of renunciation.
The past has faded, things are no longer remembered.
My sleeve is wet with tears.

～

STONE steps, a mound of lustrous green moss;
The wind carries the scent of cedar and pine.
The rain has stopped and it is beginning to clear.
I call to the children as I walk to get some village sakè.
After drinking too much, I happily write these verses.

～

POEM OF EARLY FALL

After a night of rain, water covers the village path.
This morning the thick grass by my hut is cool.
In the window, distant mountains the color of blue-green jade.
Outside, a river flows like shimmering silk.
Under a cliff near my hut, I wash out my sore ear
    with pure spring water.
In the trees, cicadas recite their fall verse.
I had prepared my robe and staff for a walk,
But the quiet beauty keeps me here.

❧

FRESH morning snow in front of the shrine.
The trees! Are they white with peach blossoms
Or white with snow?
The children and I joyfully throw snowballs.

❧

SPRING—slowly the peaceful sound
Of a priest's staff drifts from the village.
In the garden, green willows;
Water plants float serenely in the pond.
My bowl is fragrant from the rice of a thousand homes;
My heart has renounced the sovereignty of riches and
    worldly fame.
Quietly cherishing the memory of the ancient Buddhas,
I walk to the village for another day of begging.

❧

WALKING beside a clear running river, I come to a farmhouse.
The evening chill has given way to the warmth of the
morning sun.
Sparrows gather in a bamboo grove, voices fluttering
here and there.
I meet the old farmer returning to his home;
He greets me like a long-lost friend.
At his cottage, the farmer's wife heats sakè
While we eat freshly picked vegetables and chat.
Together, gloriously drunk, we no longer know
The meaning of unhappiness.

&

YESTERDAY I went to town begging food from east to west.
My shoulders are getting thinner and I cannot recall the
last time I had a heavy rice sack.
The thick frost is a continual reminder of my thin robe.
My old friends, where have they gone?
Even new faces are few.
As I walk toward the deserted summer pavilion,
Nothing but the wind of late autumn blowing through
the pines and oaks.

&

AUTUMN night—unable to sleep, I leave my tiny cottage.
Fall insects cry under the rocks, and
The cold branches are sparsely covered.
Far away, from deep in the valley, the sound of water.
The moon rises slowly over the highest peak;
I stand there quietly for a long time and
My robe becomes moist with dew.

&

RETURNING to my hermitage after filling my rice bowl,
Now only the gentle glow of twilight.
Surrounded by mountain peaks and thinly scattered leaves;
In the forest a winter crow flies.

❧

MY LIFE may appear melancholy,
But traveling through this world
I have entrusted myself to Heaven.
In my sack, three shō of rice;
By the hearth, a bundle of firewood.
If someone asks what is the mark of enlightenment
    or illusion,
I cannot say—wealth and honor are nothing but dust.
As the evening rain falls I sit in my hermitage
And stretch out both feet in answer.

One shō is about two quarts.

❧

SHAGGY hair past the ears,
A worn-out robe resembling white clouds and dark smoke.
Half drunk, half sober, I return home,
Children all around, guiding me along the Way.

❧

The wind blows through my tiny hermitage,
Not one thing is in the room.
Outside, a thousand cedars;
On the wall, several poems are written.
Now the kettle is covered with dust,
And no smoke rises from the rice steamer.
Who is pounding at my moonlit gate?
Only an old man from East Village.

                ∾

AN OLD and useless body,
I have seen many generations of flowers in this
    lonely, borrowed hermitage.
When spring comes, and if I am still alive,
Surely I will come to see you again—
Listen for the sound of my staff.

                ∾

A LONELY winter's day, clear then cloudy.
I want to go out but do not, spending some time in indecision.
Unexpectedly, an old friend comes and urges me to drink
    with him.
Joyful now, I take out the brush and ink and much paper.

                ∾

IF THERE is beauty, there must be ugliness;
If there is right, there must be wrong.
Wisdom and ignorance are complementary,
And illusion and enlightenment cannot be separated.
This is an old truth, don't think it was discovered recently.
"I want this, I want that"
Is nothing but foolishness.
I'll tell you a secret—
"All things are impermanent!"

*The last line of this poem quotes the customary formulation of the basic
doctrine of Buddhism, the most elementary and yet the most profound.*

∾

THE LONG WINTER NIGHT: THREE POEMS

The long winter night! The long winter night seems endless;
When will it be day?
No flame in the lamp nor charcoal in the fireplace;
Lying in bed, listening to the sound of freezing rain.

To an old man, dreams come easy;
I let my thoughts drift.
The room is empty and both the sakè and the oil are used up—
The long winter night.

When I was a boy studying in an empty hall,
Over and over I had to fill the lamp with oil.
Even now, that task is disagreeable—
The long winter night.

∾

GREEN mountains front and back,
White clouds east and west.
Even if I met a fellow traveler,
No news could I give him.

≈

DEEP IN the mountains at night, alone in my hermitage,
I listen to the plaintive sound of rain and snow.
A monkey cries on top of a mountain;
The sound of the valley river has faded away.
A light flickers in front of the window;
On the desk, the water in the inkstone has dried.
Unable to sleep all night,
I prepare ink and brush, and write this poem.

≈

WINTER—in the eleventh month
Snow falls thick and fast.
A thousand mountains, one color.
Men of the world passing this way are few.
Dense grass conceals the door.
All night in silence, a few woodchips burn slowly
As I read the poems of the ancients.

≈

LONELINESS: spring has already passed.
Silence: I close the gate.
From heaven, darkness; the wisteria arbor is no longer
     visible.
The stairway is overgrown with herbs
And the rice bag hangs from the fence.
Deep stillness, long isolated from the world.
All night the hototogisu cries.

The hototogisu is the so-called Japanese cuckoo.

❧

ANOTHER year lingers to an end;
Heaven sends a bitter frost.
Fallen leaves cover the mountains
And there are no travelers to cast shadows on the path.
Endless night: dried leaves burn slowly in the hearth.
Occasionally, the sound of freezing rain.
Dizzy, I try to recall the past—
Nothing here but dreams.

❧

LIGHT sleep, the bane of old age:
Dozing off, evening dreams, waking again.
The fire in the hearth flickers; all night a steady rain
Pours off the banana tree.
Now is the time I wish to share my feelings—
But there is no one.

❧

WE THROW a little woolen ball back and forth.
I don't want to boast of my skill, but . . .
If someone asks me the secret of my art, I tell him,
One, two, three, four, five, six, seven!

～

ALONE, wandering through the mountains,
I come across an abandoned hermitage.
The walls have crumbled, and there is only a path for foxes
    and rabbits.
The well, next to an ancient bamboo grove, is dry.
Spider webs cover a forgotten book of poems that lies beneath
    a window.
Dust is piled on the floor,
The stairway is completely hidden by the wild fall grasses.
Crickets, disturbed by my unexpected visit, shriek.
Looking up, I see the setting sun—unbearable loneliness.

～

THE VICISSITUDES of this world are like the movements of
    the clouds.
Fifty years of life are nothing but one long dream.
Sparse rain: in my desolate hermitage at night,
Quietly I clutch my robe and lean against the empty window.

～

DAY AFTER day after day,
The children play peacefully with this old monk.
Always two or three balls kept in my sleeves.
I have had too much to drink—spring tranquillity!

～

ZEN MASTER Ryōkan!
Like a fool, like a dunce,
Body and mind completely dropped off!

This poem has only three lines. "Body and mind completely dropped off"
refers to Dōgen's enlightenment experience. When Dōgen was practicing in
China, the monk next to him fell asleep. Dōgen's master, Tendō Nyojō
(T'ien-tung Ju-ching, 1163–1228), said in a loud voice, "Zazen is to
drop off body and mind! Why are you sleeping?" When he heard this,
Dōgen was enlightened. The expression "drop (or cast) off body and mind"
occurs frequently in Sōtō Zen literature.

∾

HOTOTOGISU

Spring has passed; the mountains and valleys are
Completely hidden in rain and mist.
In the evening the voice of the hototogisu faded,
But now, late at night, again its cry drifts
    from the bamboo grove.

∾

THE NIGHT is fresh and cool—
Staff in hand, I walk through the gate.
Wisteria and ivy grow together along the winding
    mountain path;
Birds sing quietly in their nests and a monkey
    howls nearby.
As I reach a high peak a village appears in the distance.
The old pines are full of poems;
I bend down for a drink of pure spring water.
There is a gentle breeze, and the round moon hangs overhead.
Standing by a deserted building,
I pretend to be a crane softly floating among the clouds.

∾

BEGGING

Today's begging is finished; at the crossroads
I wander by the side of Hachiman Shrine
Talking with some children.
Last year, a foolish monk;
This year, no change!

∾

Written in My Hermitage
on a Snowy Evening

For more than seventy years, I have been making
Myself dizzy observing men.
I have abandoned trying to penetrate men's good and
    bad actions.
Coming and going is a sign of weakness.
Heavy snow in the dead of night—
Under the weather-beaten window, one incense stick.

∾

Light rain—the mountain forest is wrapped in mist.
Slowly the fog changes to clouds and haze.
Along the boundless river bank, many crows.
I walk to a hill overlooking the valley to sit in zazen.

∾

After spending the day begging in town,
I now sit peacefully under a cliff in the evening cool.
Alone, with one robe and one bowl—
The life of a Zen monk is truly the best!

∾

GRASS WAR

Once again the children and I are fighting a battle using
   spring grasses.
Now advancing, now retreating, each time with more
   refinement.
Twilight—everyone has returned home;
The bright, round moon helps me endure the loneliness.

∾

LISTENING to the evening rain in my hermitage.
The Great Way? I braid spring flowers into a ball.
The future? If a visitor brings these questions
I have only the tranquillity of the hermitage to offer.

∾

A THOUSAND peaks covered with frozen snow,
Ten thousand mountain paths, yet no sign of human beings.
Every day, only zazen;
Sometimes the sound of snow blowing against the window.

∾

SUMMER NIGHT

Late at night, the faint sound of someone pounding rice.
Dew drips from the bamboo onto the firewood pile
And the plants along the garden are also moist.
Frogs croak in the distance but then seem very close.
Fireflies light low, then high.
Wide awake; sleep is far off.
Smoothing out the pillow, I let my thoughts drift.

❧

RESTING AT MATSUNO-O

The ninth month has just begun; as we walk to Matsuno-o
A solitary goose flies overhead
And the chrysanthemums are in full bloom.
The children and I have come to this pine forest.
We have only walked a short distance
But the world is hundreds of miles away.

❧

STANDING alone beneath a solitary pine;
Quickly the time passes.
Overhead the endless sky—
Who can I call to join me on this path?

❧

TWILIGHT—smoke rises from the village,
A winter goose cries overhead,
Wind blows through the mountain pines.
Alone, carrying an empty rice bowl,
I return along the path.

∾

IN THE empty doorway many petals are scattered;
As they fall they blend with the song of the birds.
Slowly, the bright spring sun appears in the window
And a thin line of smoke drifts from the incense burner.

∾

SOARING birds disappear over the distant mountains,
Leaves fall continually in the quiet garden.
Lonely autumn breezes.
An old monk in his black robe, I stand alone.

∾

LYING ill in my hermitage; all day not a single visitor.
My rice bowl has been hanging on the wall undisturbed
    for a long time,
And the wisteria has completely faded.
Dreams come, and drift over the fields and mountains.
My spirit returns to the village,
Where the children wait every day for me to come and play.

∾

THE FIREPLACE is cold, covered with thick ashes.
Again the single light has gone out.
Loneliness, and the night is only half over.
Silence—all I can hear is the voice of a distant
  mountain stream.

∾

THE SKY above, the mountains below;
Weak tea and thin soup are all I serve.
All year not one wise man,
Only an occasional woodgatherer.

∾

RETURNING home after a day of begging;
Sage has covered my door.
Now a bunch of green leaves burns together with the firewood.
Silently I read the poems of Kanzan,
Accompanied by the autumn wind blowing a light rain that
  rustles through the reeds.
I stretch out both feet and lie down.
What is there to think about? What is there to doubt?

*Kanzan (Han-shan) was a famous Chinese hermit-poet who lived around
A.D. 750. His life and poetry are highly esteemed by Zen Buddhists.*

∾

Dawn

I have returned to my native village after twenty years;
No sign of old friends or relatives—they have all died
    or gone away.
My dreams are shattered by the sound of the temple bell
    struck at sunrise.
An empty floor, no shadows; the light has long been
    extinguished.

∾

WHO SAYS my poems are poems?
My poems are not poems.
After you know my poems are not poems,
Then we can begin to discuss poetry!

∾

INTERMITTENT rain—in my hermitage
A solitary light flickers as dreams return.
Outside, the sound of falling raindrops.
A crow sits in darkness on the wall.
The fireplace is cold, no charcoal awaits my
    imagined visitors.
I reach for a volume of poems.
Tonight, in solitude, deep emotion.
How can I explain it the following day?

∾

IN FRONT of my window there is a towering banana tree,
So high it seems to sweep away the clouds.
Its shade keeps my hut cool.
As I read waka, write poems, and
Sit quietly, the day passes serenely.

～

ILLUSION and enlightenment? Two sides of a coin.
Universals and particulars? No difference.
All day I read the wordless sutra;
All night not a thought of Zen practice.
An uguisu sings in the willows along the river bank,
Dogs in the village bay at the moon.
There are no obstacles in my heart,
But still I lack a true companion.

The uguisu is the so-called Japanese nightingale.

～

MY GATE has been unbolted for many days,
Yet no sign of anyone entering the peaceful garden.
The rainy season is over, green moss is all around;
Slowly the oak leaves float to earth.

～

STAFF in hand, I walk along the river bank toward the village.
Snow lingers on the fence, but the east wind brings the first
   news of spring.
The voice of an uguisu drifts from tree to tree;
The grass has begun to show a touch of dark green.
Unexpectedly, I meet an old friend.
We converse together sitting on a hill overlooking the
   river valley.
Later, at his cottage we open many books and drink tea.
Tonight I am translating the evening scene into verse—
Plum blossoms and poetry, how wonderful together!

⌒

LYING ill again, for the third spring in a row.
How I would like just one poem left by a visitor.
Last year I played with the children all day at Hachiman Shrine.
Will they be waiting for me this year?

⌒

A LONELY four-mat hut—
All day no one in sight.
Alone, sitting beneath the window,
Only the continual sound of falling leaves.

⌒

FIRST days of spring—blue sky, bright sun.
Everything is gradually becoming fresh and green.
Carrying my bowl, I walk slowly to the village.
The children, surprised to see me,
Joyfully crowd about, bringing
My begging trip to an end at the temple gate.
I place my bowl on top of a white rock and
Hang my sack from the branch of a tree.
Here we play with the wild grasses and throw a ball.
For a time, I play catch while the children sing;
Then it is my turn.
Playing like this, here and there, I have forgotten the time.
Passers-by point and laugh at me, asking,
"What is the reason for such foolishness?"
No answer I give, only a deep bow;
Even if I replied, they would not understand.
Look around! There is nothing besides this.

❧

ON THE way to visit a famous villa several ri distant,
I unexpectedly meet a woodgatherer.
Together we walk along the narrow path hemmed in by
    green pines.
The fragrance of plum blossoms drifts from the field
    opposite the valley.
Seeking a quiet place, I have come here.
Large carp frolic in the ancient pond,
Sunlight fills the calm forest.
What is this room?
Nothing but several volumes of poetry lying on the floor.
Feeling at home, I loosen my robe
And gather a few verses from the books.
Later, at twilight, I walk along the eastern corridor as
    spring birds soar overhead.

❧

FORTY years ago, on the day of my first pilgrimage,
I struggled to draw a picture of a tiger
But it did not even resemble a cat.
Now I can see, from this mountain cliff,
The glory of the ancients scattered everywhere.

~

MY HUT lies in the middle of a dense forest;
Every year the green ivy grows longer.
No news of the affairs of men,
Only the occasional song of a woodcutter.
The sun shines and I mend my robe;
When the moon comes out I read Buddhist poems.
I have nothing to report, my friends.
If you want to find the meaning, stop chasing after
    so many things.

~

A COLD night—sitting alone in my empty room
Filled only with incense smoke.
Outside, a bamboo grove of a hundred trees;
On the bed, several volumes of poetry.
The moon shines through the top of the window,
And the entire neighborhood is still except for the cry
    of insects.
Looking at this scene, limitless emotion,
But not one word.

~

I HAVE returned to Itoigawa, my former village.
Falling ill, I rest at an inn
And listen to the sound of rain.
One robe, one bowl, are all I have.
Becoming a little stronger, I lift my weak body,
Burn some incense, and sit in zazen.
All night rain falls sadly, and
I dream of my pilgrimage these past ten years.

≈

THE INN AT TAMAGAWA STATION

Midautumn—the wind and rain are now at their most
    melancholy.
A wanderer, my spirit is inseparable from this difficult
    road.
During the long night, dreams float from the pillow—
Awake suddenly, I have mistaken the sound of the river
    for the voice of the rain.

≈

CARRYING firewood on my shoulder
I walk in the green mountains along the bumpy path.
I stop to rest under a tall pine;
Sitting quietly, I listen to the spring song of the birds.

≈

EARLY summer—floating down a clear running river in
    a wooden boat,
A lovely girl gently plays with a crimson lotus flower
    held in her white hands.
The day becomes more and more brilliant.
Young men play along the shore
And a horse runs by the willows.
Watching quietly, speaking to no one,
The beautiful girl does not show that her heart is broken.

~

SINCE I came to this hermitage
How many years have passed?
If I am tired I stretch out my feet;
If I feel fine I go for a stroll in the mountains.
The ridicule or praise of worldly people means nothing.
Following my destiny, for this body I have received
    from my parents
I have only thanks.

~

NEAR a Kannon temple, I have a temporary hermitage;
Alone, yet the intimate friend of a thousand green poems
    written on the surrounding foliage.
Sometimes in the morning I put on my priest's mantle
And go down to the village to beg food for this old body.

Kannon (Avalokitesvara) is the bodhisattva of compassion.

~

AT NIGHT, deep in the mountains I sit in zazen.
The affairs of men never reach here.
In the stillness I sit on a cushion across from the empty
    window.
The incense has been swallowed up by the endless night;
My robe has become a garment of white dew.
Unable to sleep, I walk into the garden;
Suddenly, above the highest peak, the round moon appears.

∾

DAY AND night the cold wind blows through my robe.
In the forest, only fallen leaves;
Wild chrysanthemums can no longer be seen.
Next to my hermitage there is an ancient bamboo grove;
Never changing, it awaits my return.

∾

ONCE AGAIN, many greedy people appear
No different from silkworms wrapped in cocoons.
Wealth and riches are all they love,
Never giving their minds or bodies a moment's rest.
Every year their natures deteriorate
While their vanity increases.
One morning death comes before
They can use even half their money.
Others happily receive the estate,
And the deceased's name is soon lost in darkness.
For such people there can only be great pity.

∾

MY HUT, located in a distant village, is little more than
   four bare walls.
Once I was a mendicant monk, wandering here and there,
   staying nowhere long.
Recalling the first day of my pilgrimage, years ago—
How high my spirits were!

&

THE AUTUMN nights have lengthened
And the cold has begun to penetrate my mattress.
My sixtieth year is near,
Yet there is no one to take pity on this weak old body.
The rain has finally stopped; now just a thin stream
   trickles from the roof.
All night the incessant cry of insects:
Wide awake, unable to sleep,
Leaning on my pillow, I watch the pure bright rays of sunrise.

&

KEEPING OUT OF THE RAIN

Today, while begging food, a sudden downpour.
I waited out the storm in a small shrine.
Laughing—one jug for water, one bowl for rice.
My life is like an old run-down hermitage—
   poor, simple, quiet.

&

IN THE entire ten quarters of the Buddha land
There is only one vehicle.
When we see clearly, there is no difference in all
   the teachings.
What is there to lose? What is there to gain?
If we gain something, it was there from the beginning.
If we lose anything, it is hidden nearby.
Look at the ball in the sleeve of my robe.
Surely it has great value.

The first sentence of this poem quotes a famous line from the Lotus Sutra.

∾

TRULY, I love this life of seclusion.
Carrying my staff, I walk toward a friend's cottage.
The trees in his garden, soaked by the evening rain,
Reflect the cool, clear autumnal sky.
The owner's dog comes to greet me;
Chrysanthemums bloom along the fence.
These people have the same spirit as the ancients;
An earthen wall marks their separation from the world.
In the house volumes of poetry are piled on the floor.
Abandoning worldliness, I often come to this tranquil place—
The spirit here is the spirit of Zen.

∾

LODGING at an old temple:
The night has ended, the room is empty.
The bitter cold has kept me from dreaming;
Sitting quietly, I wait for the temple bell to strike.

∾

ALWAYS, when I was a boy,
I would play here and there.
I used to put on my favorite vest
And ride a chestnut horse with a white nose.
Today I spent the morning in town
And the evening drinking amid the peach blossoms
   by the river.
Returning home, I have lost my way. Where am I?
Laughing, I find myself next to the brothel.

~

AT THE main crossroads, playing Hotei,
Coming and going with my bowl. How many years have passed?
Pretending again I do not know where I am going;
A fresh wind blows and the bright moon covers the
   autumn sky.

*Hotei (Pu-tai) was a famous Chinese sage who had an enormous belly
and traveled throughout the land carrying a large sack filled with gifts.*

~

SITTING quietly on a rough stone,
I watch clouds gather in all directions.
A golden pagoda gleams in the sun.
Below, Ryūō Spring, where one can wash both body and spirit.
Above, thousand-year-old pines.
A fresh breeze brings the day to an end.
I long to walk with another who has left the world far behind—
   but no one comes.

~

AFTER walking for a time, I reach the pavilion;
The sun sets behind the western mountains.
Willow leaves cover the little garden;
The pond is cold and the lotuses have faded.
Persimmon and chestnut trees, ripe with fruit, shade
    the path.
Along the bamboo fence, crickets cry incessantly;
Light filters easily through the pines and oaks—
Summer slowly changes its face.

EVEN IF a man lives a hundred years
His life is like a floating weed, drifting with the waves
East and west continually, no time for rest.
Shakyamuni renounced nobility and devoted his life to
Preventing others from falling into ruin.
On the earth eighty years,
Proclaiming the Dharma for fifty,
Bestowing the sutras as an eternal legacy;
Today, still a bridge to cross over to the other shore.

IF YOU speak delusions, everything becomes a delusion;
If you speak the truth, everything becomes the truth.
Outside the truth there is no delusion,
But outside delusion there is no special truth.
Followers of Buddha's Way!
Why do you so earnestly seek the truth in distant places?
Look for delusion and truth in the bottom of your own hearts.

AN EVENING dream—everything must have been an illusion;
I cannot explain clearly even one part of what I saw.
Yet in the dream it seemed as if the truth were in front
   of my eyes.
This morning, awake, is it not the same dream?

～

WALKING along a narrow path at the foot of a mountain
I come to an ancient cemetery filled with countless tombstones
And thousand-year-old oaks and pines.
The day is ending with a lonely, plaintive wind.
The names on the tombs are completely faded,
And even the relatives have forgotten who they were.
Choked with tears, unable to speak,
I take my staff and return home.

～

PEACH blossoms cover both sides of the river bank like mist.
In spring, the deep blue river appears to be the stream
   of Heaven.
Wandering here and there gazing at the peach blossoms as I
   follow the flow of the river—
What is this? An old friend's house!

～

POEM FOR A DISTANT FRIEND

Spring—late at night I go for a walk.
A trace of snow lingers on the pines and cedars.
The bright moon hangs over the mountains.
I think of you, many rivers and mountains away;
Countless thoughts, but the brush does not move.

～

THE LONG summer days at Entsū-ji temple!
Everything is fresh and pure, and
Worldly emotions never come here.
I sit in the cool shade, reading poems.
Beauty all around: I endure the heat, listening to
The sound of the water wheel.

～

SILVER-WHITE snow envelops the mountains.
Far from the village, my gate is hidden by thick weeds.
Midnight: a piece of wood burns slowly in the hearth.
An old man with a long, white, twisted beard—
My thoughts keep returning to the days of my youth.

～

EMPTY BOWL: TWO POEMS

In the blue sky a winter goose cries.
The mountains are bare; nothing but falling leaves.
Twilight: returning along the lonely village path
Alone, carrying an empty bowl.

Foolish and stubborn—what day can I rest?
Lonely and poor, this life.
Twilight: I return from the village
Again carrying an empty bowl.

∾

TO A FRIEND

The bright moon emerges over the eastern mountains.
Walking by your former house—
You are gone, yet I think of you always.
Now no one brings the koto and sakè.

*The koto is a thirteen-stringed musical instrument somewhat resembling
a zither.*

∾

WINTER NIGHT

Concealed in a dense forest, my hermitage lies far beyond
   the village river.
A thousand peaks, ten thousand mountain streams, yet no sign
   of anyone.
A long, cold winter's night—slowly a piece of wood burns
   in the fireplace.
Nothing can be heard except the sound of snow striking
   the window.

∾

WHO CAN sympathize with my life?
My hut lies near the top of a mountain,
And the path leading here is covered with weeds.
On the fence, a single gourd.
From across the river, the sound of logging.
Ill, I lie on the pillow and watch the sunrise.
A bird cries in the distance—
My only consolation.

∾

THE NUMBER of days since I left the world and
Entrusted myself to Heaven is long forgotten.
Yesterday, sitting peacefully in the green mountains;
This morning, playing with the village children.
My robe is full of patches and
I cannot remember how long I have had the same bowl
    for begging.
On clear nights I walk with my staff and chant poems;
During the day I spread out a straw mat and nap.
Who says many cannot lead such a life?
Just follow my example.

∾

FINISHING a day of begging,
I return home through the green mountains.
The setting sun is hidden behind the western cliffs
And the moon shines weakly on the stream below.
I stop by a rock and wash my feet.
Lighting some incense, I sit peacefully in zazen.
Again a one-man brotherhood of monks;
Ah . . . how quickly the stream of time sweeps by.

∾

THE ROBBER

A thief has stolen my zafu and futon.
Why did he break into my hermitage? The door is
    never locked.
The night is ending, and I sit alone by the window—
A sparse rain falls gently against the bamboo grove.

A zafu is a small round cushion used for zazen; a futon is a quilt.

BUDDHA is your mind
And the Way goes nowhere.
Don't look for anything but this.
If you point your cart north
When you want to go south,
How will you arrive?

WAKA AND HAIKU

SPRING

THEY SAY spring has come
  and the sky is filled with mist,
Yet on the mountains, no flowers, only snow.

～

AWAKENED by the cold—a light snow falls;
  the sound of wild geese.
They also are returning home with hardship and suffering.

～

STANDING on a cliff, among the pines and oaks;
  spring has come
Clothed in mist.

～

EARLY spring—picking vegetables;
  a pheasant cries—
Old memories return.

～

SPRING flows gently—
  the plum trees have bloomed.
Now the petals fall, mingling with the song of an uguisu.

～

ONLY TWO in the garden:
   plum blossoms at their peak
And an old man full of years.

∾

COUNTING days is like snapping
   one's fingers—
Even May passes like a dream.

∾

AT YAHIKO Mountain
   you can see
Both flowers and children bloom.

∾

PICKING violets by the side of the road,
   I forgot my begging bowl.
How sad you must be, my poor little bowl!

∾

I FORGOT my bowl again!
   Please, nobody pick it up,
My lonely little bowl.

∾

SPRING has begun!
   Jewels and precious gold everywhere!
Please come visit me!

∾

THE SPRING birds have all returned
    and their song drifts from every tree—
Let's have another cup of sakè.

～

TONIGHT the plum trees reflect the silver moon;
    both are in full bloom.
Entranced, I did not return home till evening.

～

EVERYWHERE you look
    the mountains are covered
With mist and blooming cherry trees.

～

HOW CAN we ever lose interest in life?
    Spring has come again
And cherry trees bloom in the mountains.

～

GOING out to beg this spring day
    I stopped to pick violets—
Oh! The day is over!

～

GAILY the warm spring days pass;
    playing with the children
In the forest below the shrine.

～

I HAVE entrusted myself to sakè and flowers:
   today sakè-sakè,
Tomorrow sakè-sakè.

In Japanese, sakè *means both rice wine (*酒*) and blooming flowers (*咲*).*

࿇

PLAYING ball with the village children
   this warm, misty spring day;
No one wants it to end.

࿇

I CAME to this village to see the peach blossoms
   but spent the day instead
Looking at the flowers along the river bank.

࿇

IN MY bowl
   violets and dandelions are mixed
Together with the Buddhas of the three worlds.

࿇

THIRSTY, I've filled myself with sakè;
   lying beneath the cherry blossoms—
Splendid dreams.

࿇

SPRING has come, the trees are in bloom,
   last autumn's leaves have disappeared—
I must hurry to meet the children.

∾

BENEATH the willows, singing and laughing
   with my friends; this fine spring day
Is truly full of joy.

∾

I EXPECTED to see only pink blossoms,
   but a gentle spring snow has fallen
and the cherry trees are wearing a white coat.

∾

HAND IN hand, the children and I
   pick spring vegetables—
What can be more wonderful?

∾

PLAYING in a garden, among the cherry trees;
   my sleeves are covered with blossoms
As the flowers fall.

∾

THE CHILDREN run to greet me
   for the first time this spring—
How they have grown!

SUMMER

IN THE distance
   frogs croak in the mountain rice fields,
The evening's single song.

∾

SUMMER evening—the voice of a hototogisu
   rises from the mountains
As I dream of the ancient poets.

∾

NOW THE farmers are planting rice;
   in my hermitage
I ask Buddha to bless them.

∾

THE RAINY season is over—it's now clear.
   I go out;
Green fields and cool breezes everywhere.

∾

UNABLE to sleep,
   I hear the voice of a young deer
Rising from a mountain ridge.

∾

THE BRANCHES that will be used for this
    autumn's firewood are still blooming.
Please gather some summer grasses, wet with dew,
    and come visit me.

❧

NOT MUCH to offer you—
    just a lotus flower floating
In a small jar of water.

❧

TRAVELING to a distant country
    accompanied by a hototogisu
And thoughts of the sadness in this world.

❧

THE CLOUDS have drifted away,
    a hototogisu cries in the brush.
Why haven't you come?

❧

I STRETCH out for a nap in my little hut.
    In the fields, frogs chant their songs
And the birds in the bamboo grove sing along.

❧

IN THE pond near my hut
    the lotus flowers, covered with dew,
Bloom in a row.

❧

WORKING with their hands, the young girls chant
   a plaintive song as they
Plant rice in the mountain fields.

❧

THE BAMBOO grove in front of my hut!
   Every day I see it a thousand times
Yet never tire of it.

❧

BACK AND forth, back and forth,
   all day the bent old man
Carries water for the parched rice seedlings.

❧

I SEEM to hear your voice in the
   song of the hototogisu.
In the mountains, another day passes.

❧

THE WILLOWS are in full bloom!
   I want to pile up the blossoms
Like mountain snow.

❧

MY HERMITAGE lies in a forest;
   all around me
Everything is thick and green.

Autumn

LONELY, I leave my hermitage;
   the rice, heavy with ripe grains,
Flutters in the autumn wind.

       ❧

PLEASE wait for the light of the moon—
   the mountain path
Is covered with fallen chestnuts.

       ❧

THE WIND has brought
   enough fallen leaves
To make a fire.

This poem is a haiku.

       ❧

A COLD autumn night—
   I clutch my white robe;
The bright, clear moon covers the sky.

       ❧

THE WIND is fresh, the moon bright.
   Let us spend the evening dancing
As a farewell to old age.

       ❧

WHILE I gather firewood and wild grasses on this hill,
   the Buddhas of the three worlds
Are also celebrating.

∽

DURING a lull in the autumn rains,
   I walk with the children along the mountain path.
The bottom of my robe becomes soaked with dew.

∽

ALONG the cedar-lined path of an old shrine
   I gather leaves
As the sun sets.

∽

WHEN IT is evening, please come to my hut
   to listen to the insects sing;
I will also introduce you to the autumn fields.

∽

TWILIGHT—crossing Kugami Mountain,
   shivering;
Fallen leaves all around.

∽

FROM TODAY the nights turn colder—
  I sew my tattered robe,
The autumn insects cry.

⁓

BRIGHT moon—I walk through the rice fields
  near my hermitage;
In the distance, mountains clothed in mist.

⁓

MORNING—cutting firewood, filling my jug
  with pure water, gathering wild grasses
While a cool autumn rain gently falls.

⁓

IF YOUR hermitage is deep in the mountains
  surely the moon, flowers, and momiji
Will become your friends.

The momiji is the Japanese maple, with small leaves that turn a brilliant crimson in autumn.

⁓

NOW THAT autumn has formed its
  first frost on my shabby robe,
It's certain no visitors will come.

⁓

I'VE LEFT the world far behind,
   my robe is covered with moss;
A small bundle of firewood burns, brightening the night.

∾

MIDAUTUMN—the mountains are crimson
   and the sakè and ink are ready,
But still no visitors.

∾

THE VILLAGE has disappeared in the evening mist
   and the path is hard to follow.
I return to my lonely hut, walking through the pines.

WINTER

DRINKING sweet sakè with the farmers
   until our eyebrows
Are white with snow.

~

RETURNING to my hermitage after a journey
   to distant mountain villages;
Along the fence, the last chrysanthemums linger.

~

LATE AT night, listening to the winter rain,
   recalling my youth—
Was it only a dream? Was I really young once?

~

THE HOUR grows late, but the sound of hail
   striking the bamboo
Keeps me from sleep.

~

ANOTHER blizzard—the mountains are
   covered with deep snow.
From now on, news from town must wait till spring.

~

I LIVE in a hut in the mountains of Echigo,
  white peaks all around.
Ice, snow, and clouds blend together.

∾

IN EVEN a light snow, we can see
  the three thousand worlds.
Again a light snow falls.

∾

WIND AND snow, then snow and rain:
  tonight, awakened by the cry of a wild goose
In the dark, endless winter sky.

∾

LYING in my freezing hut, unable to sleep;
  only the quiet roar
Of water pouring over a cliff.

∾

I WENT to see the pine at Iwamura.
  All day I stood in the rice field
Getting drenched by freezing rain.

∾

I LIE down near the hearth
  and stretch out my feet to the fire,
But still the cold pierces my belly.

∾

No begging in the town
  again today.
The snow falls and falls.

∿

Late at night, the snow
  is piling higher and higher,
Muffling the sound of the waterfall.

∿

The freezing morning rain has let up.
  What should I do?
Fetch water? Chop firewood? Gather winter greens?

∿

In the shadow of the mountains
  the firewood burns, brightening
My cold little grass hut.

∿

Winter will soon be over;
  please, please come visit
My grass hut.

∿

My heart beats faster and faster
  and I cannot sleep.
Tomorrow will be the first day of spring!

MISCELLANEOUS

THE CLOUDS are gone, the sky is clear.
  To beg food with a pure heart
Is indeed a blessing from Heaven.

∾

SINGING waka, reciting poems, playing ball
  together in the fields—
Two people, one heart.

∾

LYING on my grass pillow,
  dreaming about this dream world again—
Lonely, fitful sleep.

∾

AS I WATCH the children happily playing,
  without realizing it,
My eyes fill with tears.

∾

THINKING about the people in this floating world
  far into the night—
My sleeve is wet with tears.

∾

THE THIEF left it behind—
  the moon
At the window.

This is another haiku, Ryōkan's most famous one.

∾

WHO IS there to take pity on this old body?
  The sun sets as I return to get the staff
I left behind.

∾

PRIEST Ryōkan must fade
  like this morning's flowers,
But his heart will remain behind.

∾

WAITING for a visitor, I drank four or five
  cups of this splendid sakè.
Already completely drunk, I've forgotten who is coming.
  Next time be more careful!

∾

O, THAT my priest's robe were wide enough
  to gather up all the suffering people
In this floating world.

∾

HAVE YOU forgotten the way to my hut?
   Every evening I wait for the sound of your footsteps,
But you do not appear.

∾

IN THE vast sky the sun is setting;
   the path home is far
And the bag is already heavy.

∾

FORM, color, name, design—
   even these are things of this floating world
And should be abandoned.

∾

WHEN I think about the sadness of the people
   in this world,
Their sadness becomes mine.

∾

TWILIGHT—the only conversation
   on this hill
Is the wind blowing through the pines.

∾

THE ISLAND of Sado—
   morning and evening I often see it my in dreams,
Together with the gentle face of my mother.

∾

OUR LIVES are like the plants
   floating along the water's edge
Illumined by the moon.

         ∾

WHAT IS the heart of this old monk like?
   A gentle wind
Beneath the vast sky.

         ∾

OUR BODIES will rot and fade away,
   but the fruit of the Buddhist Law
Cannot be discarded.

         ∾

WE SEE only a straw hat and raincoat,
   but still the scarecrow
Does his job.

         ∾

TO FIND the Buddhist Law,
   drift east and west, come and go,
Entrusting yourself to the waves.

         ∾

THE SEAWEED from Nozomi near Kotoshi!
    Day and night
I dream of its wonderful taste.

∾

MONTHS pass, days pile up,
    like one intoxicated dream—
An old man sighs.

Bibliographical Note

Following are the major sources I used in preparing the translations:

Ryōkan kashū [The complete Japanese poems of Ryōkan] and Ryōkan shishū [The complete Chinese poems of Ryōkan], ed. Toyoharu Tōgō. Osaka: Sōgensha, 1973.

Other Japanese works consulted include:

Karaki, Junzō. Ryōkan. Tokyo: Chikuma Shobō, 1971.

Matsuoka, Shin'ya. Ryōkan o motomete [Searching for Ryōkan]. Tokyo: Asahi Sonorama, 1975.

Sōma, Gyofū. Daigu Ryōkan [Great Fool Ryōkan]. Tokyo: Shun'yōdō, 1918.

Tōgō, Toyoharu. Ryōkan. Tokyo: Tokyo Sōgensha, 1973.

Yoshino, Hideo. Ryōkan-oshō no hito to uta [Priest Ryōkan, the man and his poems]. Tokyo: Yayoi Shobō, 1973.

For useful references in English, see:

Fischer, Jakob. Dew-drops on a Lotus Leaf. Tokyo: 1954.

Kawabata, Yasunari. Japan the Beautiful and Myself. Trans. Edward G. Seidensticker. Tokyo, New York, and San Francisco: Kodansha International, 1968.

Suzuki, Daisetz T. Zen and Japanese Culture. Bollingen Series, vol. 64. 2nd ed. Princeton, N.J.: Princeton University Press, 1965.

Index of Titles and First Lines

Poem titles are given below in small capitals and first lines in upper and lower case.

The "weathermark" identifies this book as a production of John Weatherhill, Inc., publishers of fine books on Asia and the Pacific. Editorial supervision by Suzanne Trumbull. Book design and typography by Meredith Weatherby. Production supervision by Yutaka Shimoji. Composition by Samhwa, Seoul. Printed by Planet Press, Tokyo. Bound at the Makoto Binderies, Tokyo. The typeface used is Monotype Perpetua, with the main text in the twelve-point size.